Discarded
Kitchener Pu

NOTHING BASICALLY WRONG

More Cartoons by Pat Oliphant

Foreword by Mark Russell

Andrews and McMeel
A Universal Press Syndicate Company
Kansas City • New York

Oliphant® is syndicated internationally by Universal Press Syndicate.

Nothing Basically Wrong copyright © 1988 by Pat Oliphant. All rights reserved. Printed in the United States of America. No part of this book may be used or reproduced in any manner whatsoever without written permission except in the case of reprints in the context of reviews. For information write Andrews and McMeel, a Universal Press Syndicate Company, 4900 Main Street, Kansas City, Missouri 64112.

ISBN: 0-8362-1833-7

Library of Congress Catalog Card Number: 88-71905

—————————————————— **Attention: Schools and Businesses** ——————————————————

Andrews and McMeel books are available at quantity discounts for bulk purchase for educational, business, or sales promotional use. For information, please write to: Special Sales Department, Andrews and McMeel, 4900 Main Street, Kansas City, Missouri 64112.

Foreword

I suppose you could say that the bravery of a satirist is in direct proportion to the distance between him and his target. We can assume that at the exact moment Pat Oliphant was putting a purse into a mincing George Bush's hand, the vice-president was not in Oliphant's studio peeking over his shoulder at the time. Or, when Pat's pen instantly renders Michael Dukakis's nose to approximate a full-sized pear we know that the Duke is not sitting there posing for the portrait.

As opposed to the stand-up political humorist performing before the live, sweating party faithful in his audience, the political cartoonist need pull no punches for his own physical survival. Hell, Pat Oliphant can even walk down the street without fear of being accosted by an offended newspaper reader — "Look Edith…it's that guy what draws them awful pictures!"

Of course, it's them awful pictures that our public servants fear most — the instant, freeze-frame ridicule that once printed in a newspaper will not go away. A joke on television evaporates into the ozone layer, but a Pat Oliphant illustration lives on as a treasured keepsake of an event in the news which can turn serious people into life-sized cartoons.

Oliphant's stuff is constantly quoted, discussed, described, and reprinted — always amid torrents of laughter from Democrats and Republicans alike. Which is why I hate Pat Oliphant. But in the spirit of *perestroika* at the recent Summit Conferences between Oliphant and myself — which eventually produced the Mutually Assured Non-Plagiarizing Treaty — we agreed that I would never try to draw anything and he would never go near a piano. It seems to be working as we continue to coexist. However, when it comes to bravery there is no contest. I yield to Pat Oliphant. He is very brave — as these cartoons attest. Of course, it's easy to be brave when you work alone in a studio — and nobody knows where you live.

— MARK RUSSELL

To Grant

'WE CAN ONLY GET RONNIE REAGAN IF HE GETS TO PLAY OLLIE NORTH, SO WE'LL SIGN OLLIE TO PLAY RONNIE — WHO'LL KNOW, BABY?

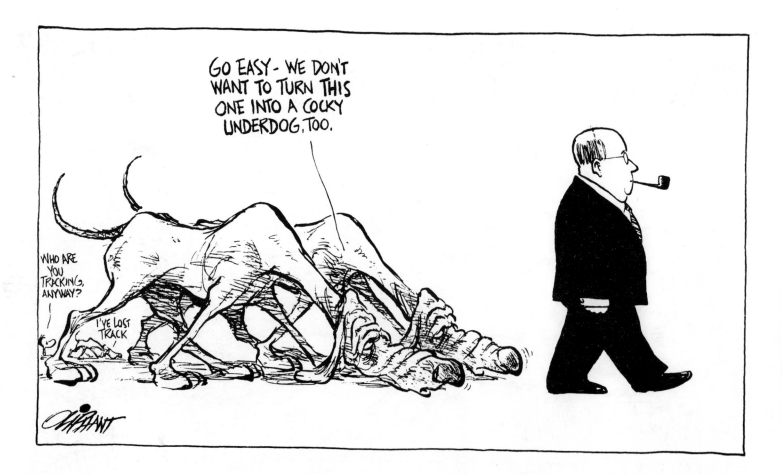

On the trail of Ollie North…and Poindexter.*

*This and all other postscripts by Pat Oliphant.

What did he know about Iran-Contra and when did he know it?

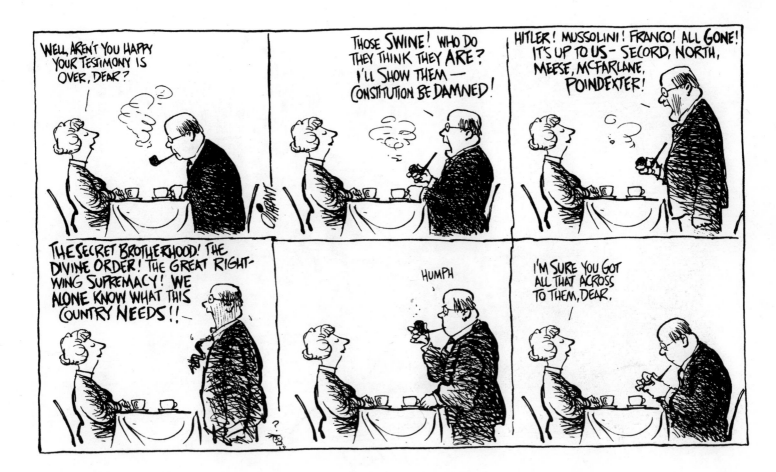

One for the "Beat the Devil" cognoscenti.

REFLAGGED.

George Shultz testifies at the Iran-Contra hearings.

July 30, 1987

NO FOOL HE, OFFICER MEESE IMMEDIATELY SUMMED UP THE SITUATION.

13

Crimebuster

YOUR DEFENSE BUDGET DOLLARS AT WORK (MINESWEEPER DIVISION).

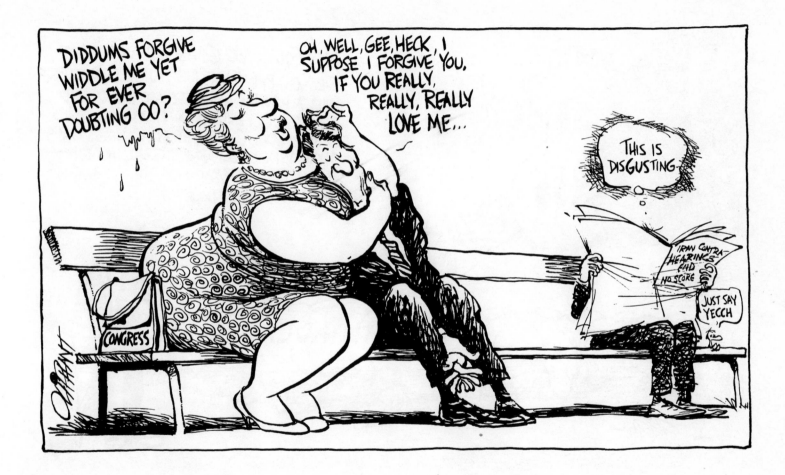

August 6, 1987

17

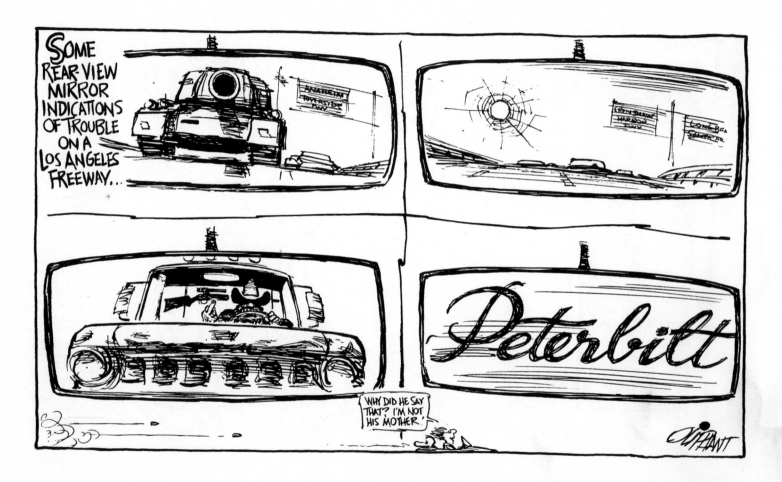

Shootings on the freeways in L.A.

Business as usual on Pennsylvania Avenue.

'..AND ANOTHER HARMONIC CONVERGENCE... AND ANOTHER HARMONIC CONVERGENCE... AND...'

RESEARCH AND DEVELOPMENT AT NASA.

August 19, 1987

22

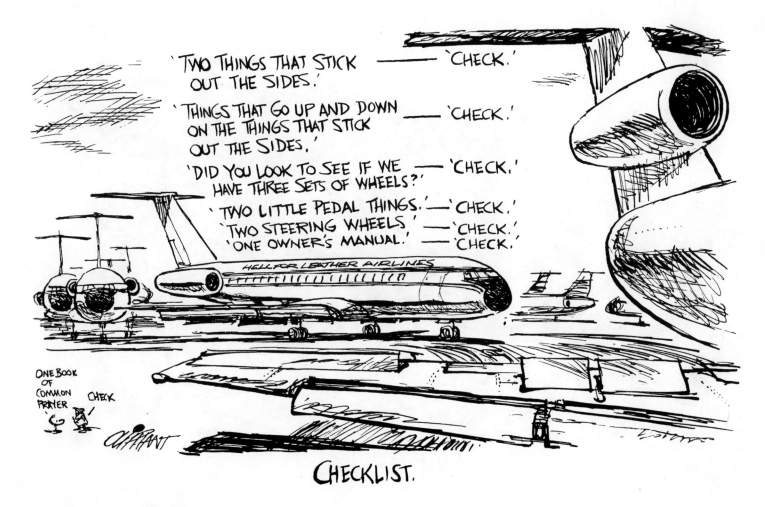

CHECKLIST.

August 24, 1987

WALLPAPER JOB.

24

Will she run in '88? Well…?

'OH, LOOK, CHILDREN – DEAR OLD UNCLE RONALD LEFT YOU THIS BOX IN HIS WILL.
WHY DON'T WE OPEN IT, AND SEE WHAT'S INSIDE...'

26

Nominee to the Supreme Court

August 27, 1987

27

'FOR ME, RE-REGULATION CAN'T COME FAST ENOUGH.'

SNOW JOB AND THE SEVEN DWARFS.

Will she run in '88? (For "dwarfs" read Dukakis, Gore, Jackson, Hart, Simon, Gephardt, Babbitt.)

September 4, 1987

33

A young German pilot lands a Cessna 172 in Moscow's Red Square.

34

SANCHO BAKER.

The papal visit grabs the American Imagination.

Old "In-Again, Out-Again" Gary Hart, back in the race.

September 14, 1987

'HEY—SOMEBODY PASS ME A BORK... OH, HI THERE, THURGOOD!'

September 15, 1987

EXTRA: TRANSPORTATION SECRETARY DOLE GIVES UP EVERYTHING TO JOIN HUSBAND'S PRESIDENTIAL CAMPAIGN.

39

September 16, 1987

BORK'S BURDEN.

Long-remembered as Nixon's errand boy

STEP ONE.

Gorbachev, Reagan

VOILA — VOODOO SCIENCE!

Quote artist, Joe Biden, decides not to run for president.

September 24, 1987

46

'I DON'T UNDERSTAND IT — WE WERE HAVING SUCH FUN...'

The Crash!...

He just hangs around the house.

GEORGE BUSH DECLARES FOR 1988: "YOU'RE GONNA SEE A REAL TIGER OUT THERE!" HE SAID.

RONALD W. REAGAN, HONORED RECIPIENT OF THE 1987 NOBEL PEACE PIE.

For his noble efforts in Central America.

October 15, 1987

55

...and the presidential reaction

'GOLLY, THIS IS THANKSGIVING! DON'T STAND OUT THERE IN THOSE OLD RAGS, STARVING AND SHIVERING WITH COLD — GO HOME!'

November 25, 1987

'WHERE ARE THOSE MEDIUM AND SHORT-RANGE MISSILES WHEN WE REALLY NEED THEM?'

THE RON AND GORBY SHOW — OR, PERHAPS, THE GORBY AND RON SHOW.

December 8, 1987

'HE SAYS IT'S A DEAL. HE DESTROYS ALL HIS MEDIUM-RANGE MISSILES, HE GETS OUT OF AFGHANISTAN, HE LETS ALL THE JEWS GO. AND YOU GIVE HIM THE SECRETS OF TEFLON.'

THE ORTEGA METHOD.

"YOU MIGHT TRY DOWN AT THE BALATA REFUGEE CAMP, BUT TRY NOT TO GET YOURSELVES SHOT BY ISRAELI SECURITY.'

December 24, 1987

67

January 4, 1988

'HERE'S HOW WE'LL HANDLE THIS BREAK-UP OF THE OZONE LAYER. WE'LL SIMPLY DOWNGRADE IT FROM "HIGHLY CARCINOGENIC" TO "MILDLY IRRITATING."'

70

KITCHENER PUBLIC LIBRARY

January 5, 1988

71

DEPORTATION — THEN AND NOW

Deep doo-doo time

'THINGS AIN'T ALL BAD – THE SHELTER ISSUED ME A WALL STREET YUPPIE TO CARRY MY BAGS.'

BOB AND GEORGE: ADVENTURES IN IOWA.

The State of the Nation

'YOU BETTER RUN ALONG WHILE YOU CAN, SIR — IF MR. BUSH HEARS THAT QUESTION ONE MORE TIME, I'M AFRAID WE MAY NOT BE ABLE TO RESTRAIN HIM!'

78

The tiger is loose. The question: "What do you know about the Iran-Contra affair?"

'ANOTHER DEAD SKUNK! SUCH A CLEVER DOGGIE, EDDIE!'

February 2, 1988

'ONE LAST REQUEST... I WANT YOU GUYS IN CONGRESS TO GET OUT THERE AND KILL ONE MORE COMMIE FOR THE GIPPER.'

80

SPEAKING OF GUN CONTROL...

New Hampshire primary time

February 11, 1988

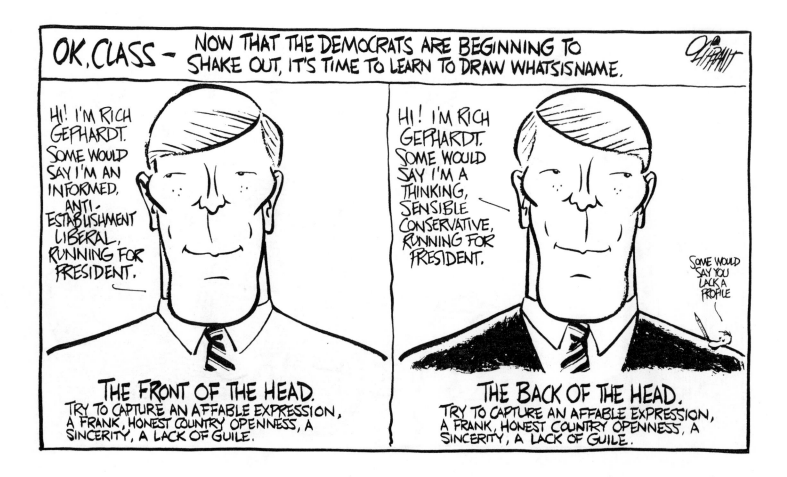

Panama! Noriega named a drug-runner.

February 23, 1988

89

Sorry, wrong number. But who cares?

A landmark decision by the Supreme Court. If Falwell had prevailed, this book would have ended on the previous page.

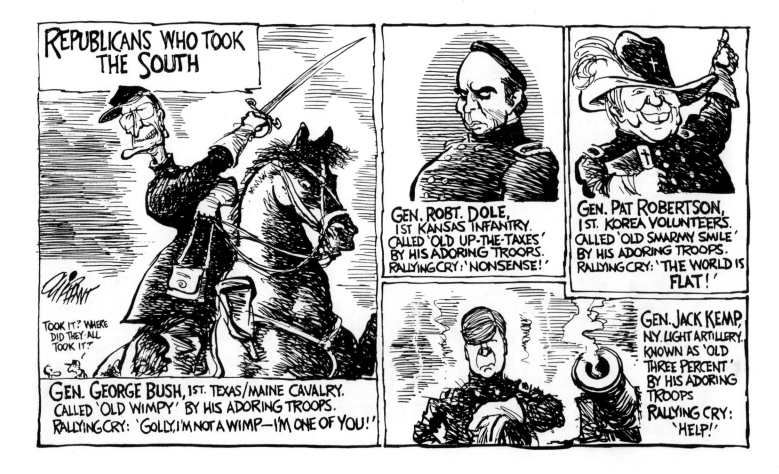

DEMOCRATS WHO TOOK THE SOUTH

GEN. MICHAEL DUKAKIS, IST. MASSACHUSETTS POLITICAL ENGINEERS. KNOWN AS 'OLD CARPETBAG' BY HIS ADORING TROOPS. RALLYING CRY: 'I'M NOT EVEN ONE OF YOU.'

I AIN'T MUCH TOOK BY ANY UV 'EM!

GEN. RICH^{D.} GEPHARDT, IST. POPULIST RESERVES, KNOWN AS 'OLD FLIP-FLOP' BY HIS ADORING TROOPS. RALLYING CRY: 'WHAT DO YOU WANT TO HEAR?'

GEN. JESSE JACKSON, IST. EVANGELICAL VOLUNTEERS, 'OLD KINGMAKER' TO HIS ADORING TROOPS. RALLYING CRY: 'I AIN'T ONE OF YOU BUT YOU CAN CALL ME 'SIR'!'

GEN. ALBERT GORE, 2ND. TENN. INFANTRY, KNOWN TO HIS ADORING TROOPS AS 'OLD WHATSISNAME.' RALLYING CRY: 'WHERE'S THE MAP?'

GEN. GARY HART, IST. COLO. REVOLUNTEERS, KNOWN TO HIS ADORING TROOPS AS 'OLD NEW IDEAS'. ALSO KNOWN AS 'OLD MONKEY BUSINESS'. RALLYING CRY: 'WHERE'S THE BIMBOS?'

General, here's your hat. Weren't you leaving…?

'WOULD YOU SAY YOU ARE Ⓐ OPPOSED TO AN ACCORD? ⒷTOTALLY OPPOSED? ©ADAMANTLY OPPOSED? Ⓓ VIOLENTLY OPPOSED?'

March 3, 1988

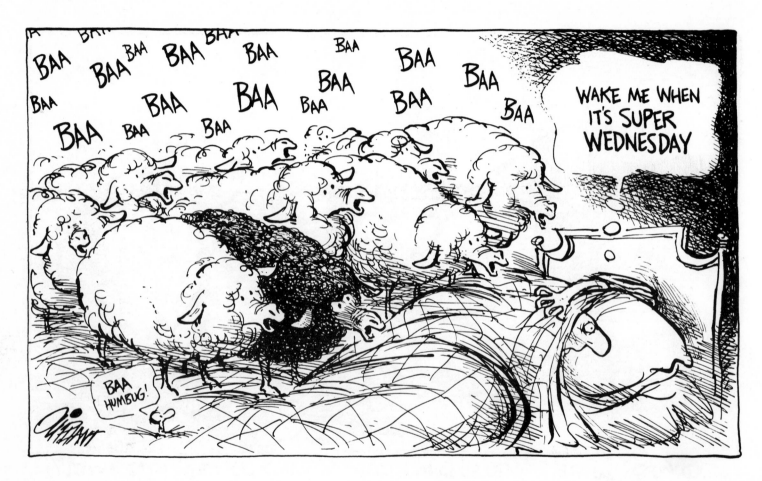

96

Super Tuesday, the Day of Primaries

Jesse on a roll.

'HEY, THAT'S CUTE! WHAT ELSE CAN IT DO?'

March 15, 1988

103

Deny you were ever *at* the White House.

One primary does not a campaign make.

March 18, 1988

106

On and on and on…

The tiger is still loose.

Jackson is doing *too* well.

March 30, 1988

114

'HEY, WADDAYOU DOIN' HERE? AIN'T YOU DA WISA GUY BEEN TAKIN' ALLA DA CREDIT FOR NAILIN' US ONNA DIS DRUG-RUNNIN' RAP?'

Meese claims credit for a big Mafia drug bust. However…

Just remembering, Jesse…

Hands off, gringo. Don't get tough with a brother.

HEAD TABLE

April 8, 1988

'OK, IF YOU WON'T READ IT TO ME, I'LL READ IT MYSELF.'

121

AT A TIME OF GREAT NATIONAL BOREDOM, THE PEOPLE SEARCH FOR REASSURANCE...

Who wants to inherit the Reagan years?

April 13, 1988

BATTERIES NOT INCLUDED

The omnipotent IRS

Air exchange in the Persian Gulf

April 21, 1988

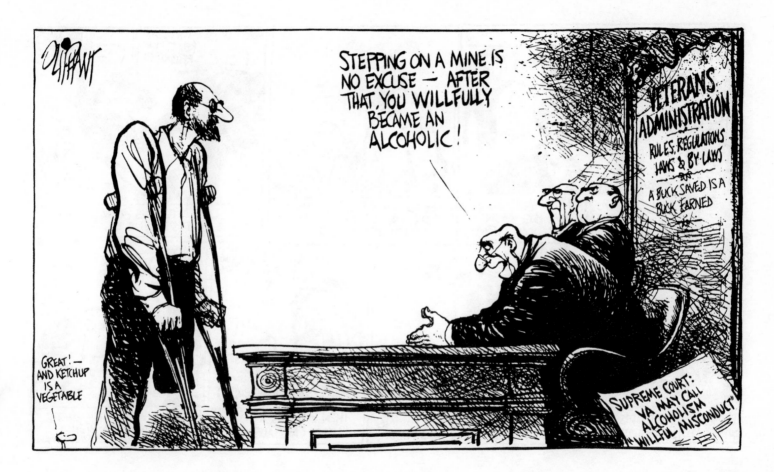

127

April 26, 1988

Meese stays on.

'IT'S MORNING IN AMERICA, SIR, AND THE PAPERS SAY IT'S TIME TO GET OUT OF BED, SHARPEN YOUR IMAGE, STEAL A LITTLE FROM JACKSON, AND GET DOWN AND DIRTY WITH THE WORLD.'

FIRST DATE.

'GOSH, GENERAL NORIEGA, HOW **DO** YOU DO IT? A PAIR OF **TWO**s! BEAT ME AGAIN.'

May 4, 1988

PERESTROIKA

136

May 8, 1988

138

Alien invaders from outer space would surely unite the world, said the president, all this during his Astrology Period.

May 11, 1988

A BEAUTY CONTEST: THE PRELIMINARIES.

May 12, 1988

THE WIZARD WHO DID.

141

All Ed Meese asked for in his staff was loyalty. Why did they all leave?

THE FACTS OF LIFE AND DEATH IN THE EXECUTIVE SUITE.

May 19, 1988

146

Federal officials may search for evidence in your garbage.

May 23, 1988

148

FINAL BRIEFING.

House astrologer is moved to cabinet level.

Birds can't talk. Except, perhaps, the Noriega parrot. Sometimes.

Reagan in Moscow II

THE DRAGON SLAYERS.

June 9, 1988

154

'HALT IN THE NAME OF THE LAW OF REAGANOMICS!'

June 16, 1988

SOME EPITAPHS.

Court awards damages to smoker who died of cigarette-induced cancer.

A HOME WHERE THE BUFFALO ROAM.

Anti-gun columnist shoots intruder with unregistered pistol.

THE FARM GAME

'GOOD LORD, NUMM-SMYTHE — WHAT WAS THAT?'

Women in clubs? What next!

'PLEASE, POPPA GORBACHEV. I'M TOO YOUNG TO GO OUT ON MY OWN. YOU KNOW I DON'T HAVE ANY INITIATIVE, YOU'VE SAID SO YOURSELF. WHO'LL LOOK AFTER ME? I'LL STARVE, POPPA.'

'THERE'S NO POLICY SO FLAWED, GEORGE, THAT CAN'T BE FIXED BY THROWING MORE MONEY AT IT!'

Iranian airliner downed by U.S. ship. Money offered in compensation.

165

Sen. Lloyd Bentsen of Texas is V.P. candidate.

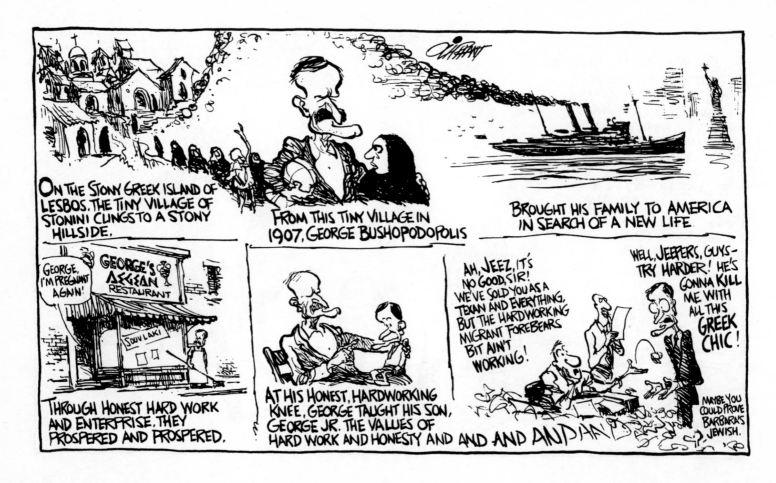

July 22, 1988

'STOP, IN THE NAME OF HUMANITY. BESIDES, I'M LOSING.'

'GOLLY — HOW CAN THEY SAY THAT?'

237175

COVERT MOVES ARE BEING PLANNED AGAINST NORIEGA...